INSIGHT IGNITED: ACTIVE LEARNING IN A DISENGAGED WORLD

THE SURPRISING CONNECTION BETWEEN BETTER CLASSROOMS AND BETTER WORKPLACES

BY PAULA RAYMOND STAMP, PH.D.

Published by **Geaux Consulting Group Publishing**

Library of Congress Control Number: *2026902308*

ISBN (Hardcover): *979-8-9946901-2-3*
ISBN (Paperback): *979-8-9946901-0-9*
ISBN (E-book): *979-8-9946901-1-6*

Cover design by *Tram8x*
Interior design and layout by *Tram8x*

This book is a work of nonfiction. Examples, scenarios, and case descriptions are used for illustrative purposes and do not depict actual individuals or organizations unless specifically noted.

For permissions or inquiries, contact:
Geaux Consulting Group Publishing
www.geauxconsultinggroup.com

Printed in the United States of America

Dedication

To Tyler and Nia

Contents

Contents

Prologue

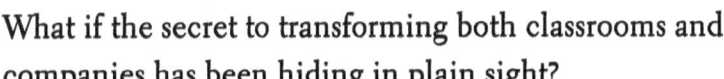

What if the secret to transforming both classrooms and companies has been hiding in plain sight?

In Insight Ignited, Paula Raymond Stamp, Ph.D. bridges two worlds rarely discussed together: the undergraduate classroom and the modern workplace. Drawing from her academic research, industry experience, and years of consulting with leaders, she shows how the principles of active learning, long celebrated in higher education, hold the key to solving today's engagement crisis in business.

Across chapters that blend storytelling, research, and practical frameworks, Paula explores why people disengage, what environments pull them back in, and how student-faculty interaction, motivation, culture, leadership behavior, and person-environment fit shape the way we learn, work, and connect. With clarity and insight, she explores the physical spaces where learning happens, the cultures that bring people together, and the interpersonal interactions that elevate performance. From mindfulness and deep learning to organizational trust and team dynamics, she makes a compelling case: when learning spaces are designed intentionally, people show up differently.

Whether you're a faculty member trying to reach your students, a manager trying to retain talent, or a leader ready to build a healthier culture, this book offers a new lens for understanding human engagement. You'll discover how small behavioral shifts, redesigned physical environments, and more meaningful interpersonal interactions ignite better thinking and better results.

Insight Ignited is an essential read for educators, executives, and anyone committed to building spaces where people thrive.

Engagement is not a tactic. It's an architecture.

And when we design it well, everything improves.

Introduction

The year was 1999. During one of my early semesters of teaching, I stood before a room of college business students who were bright and capable, but disengaged. I was barely older than they were, yet I was expected to impart knowledge to them. The discussion prompt I had spent hours crafting landed with a soft thud. Eyes glazed over. Attention drifted. The room felt heavy, and I was unsure how to move forward.

Years later, I realized the problem was not my content. It was the way I had designed the learning experience. I had created a course that delivered information rather than invited participation.

So, I changed my lesson plan. We added more group activities and even planned a major event for the city as a class. Participation and engagement improved, but something was still missing.

Several years later, during a training workshop for a large general construction firm, I witnessed the same silence in a corporate setting instead of a classroom. Technical staff sat in perfect rows, waiting to be taught how to engage clients. The energy was the same: compliance without connection.

During that training, I shifted my approach again. We formed small groups, encouraged intimate discussions, invited participants to teach one another, and asked the question, "What does engagement look like here?" Within minutes, the room was alive with conversation and organic learning was taking place.

Those moments, separated by years and industries, revealed a shared truth: whether in academic or corporate environments, engagement is not accidental; it's by design. It is created intentionally through choices that honor curiosity, autonomy, and relationships.

This book is about that kind of design. It is about how learning, leadership, and culture are built from the inside out, and how systems, spaces, and relationships shape the energy that allows organizations and classrooms to thrive. It is about what becomes possible when we stop treating engagement as a metric and start treating it as an experience.

The Architecture of This Book

The book is based on an empirical study that explored whether active learning pedagogy contributes to first-year undergraduate students' engagement in the learning process. The study data was collected at the beginning of the semester of a freshman seminar course and again at the end. The dataset included self-reported responses to a survey administered to first-year undergraduate students and to faculty teaching a freshman seminar at a private, four-year university. The analysis of this data was undertaken as part of my doctoral dissertation.

Why are the outcomes of this study important? The findings proved valuable not only in higher education settings but in corporate environments as well. Layering student responses with faculty insight closely aligned with how employees and supervisors collaborate in organizational settings. The outcomes have broad implications for how companies understand leadership, employee engagement, and the design of physical environments that promote both. This book will explore that intersection.

The book is organized not as a linear argument but as a living structure, presented as a series of connected spaces that invite participation and reflection. Each chapter builds on the last, mirroring the evolution of engagement itself, moving from theory to practice and from individual energy to collective design.

The early chapters lay the foundation. They challenge traditional ideas about teaching, leadership, and learning by asking a simple question: *What if the way we communicate and the spaces we occupy determine how deeply people engage?*

- Chapter 1 examines the lecture as a symbol of passive learning, revealing how real engagement begins when learners and leaders share responsibility for discovery.

- Chapter 2 reframes faculty and leadership engagement as catalysts for culture, positioning teaching and management as parallel forms of influence.

- Chapter 3 shifts from individuals to systems, exploring how organizations and institutions can redesign the architecture of engagement itself.

From there, the book expands outward, connecting psychology, design, and practice:

- Chapter 4 explores the architecture of energy and the motivational and mindful design elements that make learning spaces come alive.

- Chapter 5 turns theory into motion through active learning pedagogy, showing how intentional design transforms passivity into participation.

- Chapter 6 examines the physical and digital environments that either amplify or silence engagement, reminding us that space is an active teacher.

- Finally, Chapter 7 moves beyond data to human connection, illustrating how relationships become the agent for belonging and legacy.

This progression from reflection to action and from structure to spirit mirrors the journey of any organization or classroom seeking deeper engagement.

What This Book Asks of You

Engagement, at its essence, is an invitation. So is this book.

You are invited not to agree with every idea but to interact with them; to question, adapt, and apply. Whether you are an educator reimagining the classroom or a leader redesigning organizational culture, you are a builder of human experience.

Each chapter offers both a mirror and a blueprint. The mirror reflects where you are; the blueprint suggests where you might go next.

A Reflective Beginning

The evolution of engagement is, by design, never static. It is built, tested, and rebuilt through relationships, curiosity, and care. As you begin this journey, I invite you to read intently, think deeply, and notice connections between students and teams, between learning and leading, between your own energy and the systems you influence.

In every chapter, you'll find ideas to apply, stories to inspire, and questions to challenge your assumptions. But above all, I hope you find confirmation of something timeless: that the way we design our environments, our relationships, and our choices can change not only how people learn but how they live.

Welcome to the blueprint.

Balance insight with application, theory with design, and scholarship with storytelling.

How to Use This Book

••●→❀←●••

This book was designed to be interactive. Not in the sense of worksheets or exercises, but through rhythm, reflection, and dialogue. Every chapter is a conversation between the two worlds of education and business with each informing the other.

Throughout the book, you'll find four recurring call-out features that serve as directional elements of the reading experience:

- *Teaching Insight* shares research-grounded perspectives on engagement, motivation, and learning design with clarity drawn from decades of scholarship.

- *Leadership Parallel* bridges the theory to practice, connecting faculty behaviors to leadership dynamics within organizations. These sections show that good teaching *is* good leadership and vice versa.

- *From the Classroom to the Boardroom* illustrates how academic insights translate to business environments, reinforcing the idea that engagement is universal across context.

- *Engagement Tip* distills practical wisdom into short, actionable takeaways comprised of small design interventions that make big differences in how people connect and participate.

This book follows a rhythm that ebbs and flows between teaching and learning. Each chapter moves through a cycle of concept, story, insight, and application. You will encounter brief **illustrative**

vignettes that include snapshots of classrooms, teams, and organizations, grounding theory in human experience. These vignettes are not meant to be copied but are intended to spark ideas and possibilities on your campus or within your organization. Although they are fictional, they are designed to translate into meaningful and relatable outcomes.

This rhythm reflects active learning itself: read, reflect, act, refine. Just as the most engaging classrooms thrive through iteration, this book invites you to move between reflection and experimentation, between thinking and doing. It is not intended to be read in a single sitting but explored like a learning environment that reveals new insights each time you return.

You'll also notice that each chapter ends with two recurring elements: a *reflective synthesis* and a *practical framework*. The reflective section invites you to pause and process what you've read. You are being asked to consider not just the ideas, but how they resonate with your own experience. The framework then provides a bridge to action: specific, evidence-informed strategies for redesigning systems, spaces, and relationships.

Think of these features as the book's architectural supports; the load-bearing structures that balance insight with application, theory with design, and scholarship with storytelling.

CHAPTER 1

The Echo Chamber

Why Talking Isn't Teaching

Walk into almost any lecture hall or corporate training room and you will recognize the choreography. The speaker stands centered, confident and composed, while rows of chairs face forward in quiet obedience. Slides flicker. Pens hover. The ritual begins. For an hour or two, words spill out in a practiced rhythm, occasionally interrupted by a rhetorical question that no one answers.

It feels clinical, controlled, safe. Yet beneath the symmetry of rows and the glow of PowerPoint lies a paradox. The more one person speaks, the less everyone else learns. The traditional lecture, whether in a freshman classroom or an executive retreat, has become an echo chamber of information that moves in only one direction and too often leaves participants applauding instead of applying.

We hold on to the lecture because it promises efficiency: one expert, many listeners, measurable coverage. However, education, and by extension organizational learning, should not be transactional. It is a human exchange. The echo chamber reassures the speaker while isolating the learner.

The Myth of Efficiency

For centuries, efficiency has been the lecture's guiding principle. It organizes knowledge into neat sequences, allows control of time and topic, and fits comfortably within institutional schedules. Goffe and Kauper (2014) found that many faculty rely on lectures precisely because they streamline preparation and ensure coverage. Corporate trainers repeat the pattern for similar reasons: fewer surprises, consistent messaging, and accessible metrics.

Yet learning is rarely efficient. It is messy, iterative, and social. Doll and colleagues (2010) describe engaged environments as those that nurture supportive interaction, foster ownership of learning, and build confidence in success. These qualities require dialogue, not download.

Freeman and colleagues (2014) quantified what many educators sensed intuitively. In a meta-analysis of 225 studies, they found that students in active learning environments scored 6 percent higher on exams and were 1.5 times less likely to fail. These are not marginal improvements; they signal a redefinition of success.

In business settings, the same pattern holds. A one-way town hall briefing may fulfill communication protocols, yet it rarely sparks behavioral change. Organizations, like classrooms, often confuse exposure with engagement. The assumption that hearing information equates to learning remains as flawed in boardrooms as it is in lecture halls.

Active learning operates differently. It shifts responsibility. It asks participants to process, question, and create. It transforms learning from a spectator activity into a participatory one.

Teaching Insight: Control comforts instructors but constrains learners. Real learning trades certainty for discovery.

The Cost of Disconnection

If the lecture persists, it is partly because the systems supporting it remain inequitable. The National Assessment of Educational Progress (2024) reported that only 22 percent of eighth-grade students were proficient in math, 31 percent in science, and 35 percent in reading. By high school, progress plateaus. Only 20 percent of ACT-tested students meet readiness benchmarks (ACT, 2025).

These numbers conceal deeper disparities. Underrepresented students, including Black, Latino, and Indigenous learners, experience under-resourced schools, limited access to advanced coursework, and cultural disconnection in pedagogy (Contreras, 2011). Harper (2012) found that Black male students report significantly lower academic engagement and preparation. From 1990 to 2013, bachelor's degree attainment gaps between White students and their peers of color widened (Kena et al., 2014).

The result is not simply uneven achievement; it is alienation. Students absorb the message that classrooms were not built for them. Rows of chairs and the elevated podium reinforce hierarchy, signaling that participation must be granted rather than expected.

Engagement Tip: Belonging precedes achievement. When learners recognize themselves in the environment, both physically and culturally, they invest more deeply in the process.

The business world mirrors this dynamic. Companies tout inclusion yet deliver training in spaces or virtual platforms that mute diverse voices. When meetings are dominated by a few and structured for compliance, innovation suffers. The geometry of engagement is universal: circles invite, rows divide.

Schreiner (2010b) argued that surface indicators such as attendance or note-taking misrepresent engagement. When evaluation focuses on cognitive investment, such as curiosity, persistence, collaboration, gender and cultural gaps narrow. In both universities and organizations, engagement thrives where individuals feel seen and heard.

Grades or performance scores, meanwhile, measure output, not insight. For first-generation students or early-career professionals, these metrics often trail reality, registering struggle rather than potential. More predictive of persistence are relational factors like connection, mentorship, and community (Hausmann, Schofield, & Woods, 2007).

From the Lecture Hall to the Learning Lab: Metrics don't create meaning. Engagement grows from relationships that humanize data.

From Mentorship to Management...and Back Again

In Reformation-era Europe, tutors lived with their pupils, and learning was conversational and communal (Altbach, Gumport, and Berdahl, 2011). Early American colleges carried that intimacy forward, viewing education as a process of moral formation. Higher education once understood this instinctively.

Industrialization, however, transformed both the economy and the classroom. As factories prioritized specialization and productivity, universities mirrored the model. By the late nineteenth century, the German research university had become the gold standard. Faculty aligned with disciplines rather than students, and teaching lost status to publishing (Cohen and Kisker, 2010). The lecture hall emerged as a symbol of modernity, with its orderly, efficient, and hierarchical structure.

In the twentieth century, universities adopted corporate structures, and corporate America, ironically, adopted the lecture. Boardrooms became auditoria in miniature. Whether discussing quarterly results or quantum theory, the posture was identical: the front speaks, the back listens.

Data again challenges tradition. Research by Lundberg and Schreiner (2004) confirms that student-faculty interaction strongly predicts learning and persistence, particularly for students of color. Yet institutional reward systems continue to privilege research output over relational teaching. Faculty, much like middle managers, find themselves pulled toward metrics that quantify everything except connection.

Business leaders face the same tension. Performance reviews, dashboards, and quarterly goals measure productivity but rarely capture learning. When organizations separate development from dialogue, they create knowledge workers who lack mentorship.

The solution is not to abandon rigor but to restore reciprocity. Teachers and leaders must move from transmission to translation and from telling to co-creating understanding.

Teaching Insight: Presence is the pedagogy. A few moments of genuine interaction outweigh hours of polished delivery.

Reimagining Engagement

To close the echo chamber, we must redesign both the method and the mindset. In classrooms, this means integrating practices that promote autonomy, competence, and relatedness, the same psychological drivers of engagement identified in self-determination theory. In organizations, it means creating environments where employees experience ownership, mastery, and connection.

Active learning pedagogy offers a different blueprint. Its principles extend beyond academia into every arena where people gather to grow. Discussion replaces dictation; collaboration replaces compliance.

Consider the subtle shift in a faculty meeting or a leadership workshop when the facilitator asks, "What patterns do you notice?" instead of "Does everyone understand?" The first question invites exploration, while the second tests obedience. Language signals an invitation to dialogue.

In both education and enterprise, the future of engagement depends on designing systems that value curiosity as much as content. This requires courage, the willingness to slow down, to listen longer, and to risk not knowing.

———————— •••••• ————————

Engagement Tip: Ask for discovery, not agreement. The question you pose determines the depth of thinking you receive.

———————— •••••• ————————

Reflection: Breaking the Echo

The enduring appeal of the lecture isn't ignorance but inertia. It promises control in a world that resists it. But learning, by nature, is a conversation. Whether in a freshman seminar or a strategy retreat, transformation occurs only when knowledge becomes shared experience.

We are, in the end, social learners. Our brains are wired for connection, not consumption. The goal is not to silence the expert but to multiply expertise and to create spaces where voices resonate rather than reverberate.

———————— •••••• ————————

From the Lecture Hall to the Learning Lab: Teaching and leadership converge where dialogue begins.

———————— •••••• ————————

Framework for Action: Moving from Echo to Engagement

1. **Redefine Success.** Measure interaction, not airtime. Evaluate how often learners speak, question, and apply not how much content is covered.

2. **Design for Dialogue.** Rearrange spaces, both physical or virtual, so participants face each other. Circles signal collaboration.

3. **Model Curiosity.** Replace statements with open-ended questions; model learning as a shared act.

4. **Empower Participants.** Give learners choices in process or pacing. Autonomy fuels investment.

5. **Sustain the Conversation.** Engagement is a cultural mindset. Embed feedback loops that keep dialogue alive beyond the event.

Reimagining engagement starts with dismantling the illusion that talking equals teaching. But once the noise quiets and conversation begins, a deeper question emerges: *How do we design systems that make engagement sustainable rather than situational?*

Chapter 2 explores the structures, cultures, and leadership behaviors that turn isolated moments of active learning into enduring institutional practice.

CHAPTER 2

The Catalyst Effect

---•→✦←•---

How Faculty (and Business Leaders) Shape the Culture of Learning

T he end of the lecture is not the end of teaching. It's the beginning of leadership. In the previous chapter, we dismantled the myth that learning is a one-way street. But if learning is a conversation, someone must model how to keep that dialogue alive. That role belongs to the teacher or, in organizational terms, the leader. Both hold a similar mandate: to turn potential into performance, curiosity into capability, and individuals into collaborators.

Faculty engagement, much like leadership engagement in business, is the catalyst that determines whether a culture of learning thrives or fades. When teachers lead with presence and purpose, classrooms transform. When leaders teach with empathy and curiosity, organizations do too. The catalyst is not policy, but it's people.

The Power of Presence

Faculty engagement begins with something deceptively simple: being fully present.

In higher education, the professionalization of faculty has often fragmented that presence. The rise of research expectations, publication metrics, and grant acquisition, especially following the twentieth-century shift toward the German research model, has made scholarly output the primary currency for tenure. Teaching, once central to academic identity, has become a secondary conversation.

The result is not only procedural, but cultural. Many institutions, and by extension many faculty members, define success through disciplinary recognition rather than through student achievement. Their workdays are spent producing knowledge rather than facilitating it. Meanwhile, the relational energy that fuels learning, such as feedback, conversation, and mentorship, diminishes.

Yet when faculty reengage as leaders in their classrooms, the difference can be profound. Schreiner and Louis (2011) found that engaged faculty demonstrate the same intrinsic motivation seen in engaged students. They experience meaning not only in the material they teach, but in the growth of those they teach. Their classrooms become places of possibility. Questions linger longer, curiosity deepens, and confidence expands.

The same dynamic applies in organizations. Leaders who treat employees as co-learners rather than subordinates unlock collective intelligence. Just as engaged faculty amplify student engagement, engaged leaders elevate team performance. In both cases, presence centers on meaningful participation.

When teachers and managers model genuine investment, they build cultures of trust. That trust becomes the foundation for risk-taking, experimentation, and ultimately, innovation.

———————— •◦●◆●◦• ————————

Teaching Insight: Presence precedes pedagogy. The best curriculum cannot compensate for an absent teacher or leader.

———————— •◦●◆●◦• ————————

From Expertise to Influence

Expertise may earn authority, but engagement earns influence. Historically, faculty have been trained to see their authority as intellectual and to lecture from mastery, not to learn alongside. Yet the most effective teachers and leaders recognize that expertise is not diminished by humility; it's magnified by it.

Livingston (2011) found that faculty who are connected to their teaching process demonstrate greater adaptability and responsiveness. Their students report higher satisfaction and deeper learning. These outcomes are not the result of perfect course design but of relational agility and faculty adjusting in real time to student needs.

———————— •◦●◆●◦• ————————

Leadership Parallel: Authority without empathy is management. Authority with empathy is leadership.

———————— •◦●◆●◦• ————————

In business environments, this principle drives some of the most successful learning cultures. At companies such as Pixar and IDEO, leaders act as creative catalysts, guiding teams through inquiry rather than delivering predetermined solutions. In much the same way, the active learning classroom positions the professor as a facilitator and co-explorer. The hierarchy of knowledge gives way to a network of curiosity.

Research by Kim and Sax (2017) shows that faculty-student interaction, particularly for underrepresented students, has a significant impact on motivation and academic success. When students perceive instructors as invested and approachable, their performance improves. Likewise, in organizations, employees who view leaders as accessible and committed report higher engagement and lower turnover. Engagement increases wherever empathy and expertise meet.

From the Classroom to the Boardroom: Whether mentoring a first-year student or onboarding a new hire, the principle is the same: people commit to learning when they sense that their growth matters to someone in charge.

The Flow of Engagement

Faculty engagement isn't merely behavioral. It is emotional and cognitive. Nakamura and Csikszentmihalyi (2005) described how faculty who experience "flow" in teaching, the deep, immersive focus that makes work intrinsically rewarding, become more open, creative, and connected. When educators reach this state, students sense it. The classroom energy becomes contagious.

Flow is not accidental; it is shaped through autonomy, mastery, and connection. These are the same drivers that motivate employees in high-performing organizations. Engaged faculty feel ownership over their teaching, competence in their methods, and relational connection to students. Engaged leaders feel ownership of their culture, confidence in their purpose, and connection to their teams.

When these conditions align, performance accelerates. Research by Schreiner and Louis (2011) found that mutual engagement between faculty and students fosters deeper learning outcomes and satisfaction on both sides. Faculty describe renewed joy in teaching. Students report renewed interest in learning. The effect is reciprocal, as each fuels the other.

Engagement Tip: Energy transfers through attention. Where teachers and leaders direct their focus, others follow.

For underrepresented students and employees alike, engaged mentorship can be transformational. Cole (2010) noted that when faculty-student interaction centers on challenge and feedback, achievement among underrepresented groups improves significantly. Similarly, organizations that intentionally mentor emerging leaders from underrepresented backgrounds see higher retention and performance. Engagement, then, becomes an act of inclusion.

Designing the Conditions for Connection

True engagement requires an intentional approach. Faculty often cite barriers: large classes, inflexible spaces, limited training, and the tyranny of time. Yet these challenges are not insurmountable. They can be addressed by looking at them through the lens of space design.

Kuh (2003) defined involvement as the time and energy students devote to educational activities. Faculty shape that involvement by how they structure interaction. The same applies to leadership.

Managers who create opportunities for collaboration, such as short debriefs, reflective sessions, and shared problem-solving, shape engagement by design.

Active learning pedagogy offers one solution. When faculty adopt strategies that invite participation through the use of case studies, simulations, and peer instruction, they transform passive students into co-creators. Bonwell and Eisen (1991) found that these methods develop higher-order thinking, while Umbach and Wawrzynski (2004) showed that faculty who use these techniques promote both cognitive and affective engagement.

Teaching Insight: Active learning is leadership in motion. It converts knowledge into experience and followers into participants.

However, engagement doesn't mean chaos. Michel, Carter, and Varela (2009) caution that effectiveness depends on intentional design. The same is true in corporate contexts. "Agile" meetings or creative brainstorming only work when facilitated with clarity and purpose. The best leaders and teachers balance structure with freedom.

Institutional and organizational support amplify this balance. Centers for Teaching and Learning, leadership development programs, and coaching systems all act as scaffolds that sustain engagement. When organizations invest in professional growth, they send a signal: learning is culturally valued.

———————•••••———————

From the Classroom to the Boardroom: When leaders prioritize continuous learning, they transform compliance cultures into growth cultures. The message shifts from "perform" to "develop."

———————•••••———————

The Human Multiplier

At its core, faculty engagement is a human multiplier. Engaged teachers create conditions for others to engage, while disengaged teachers dampen curiosity. The same equation applies to leadership. Engagement cascades downward.

Chickering and Gamson (1987) noted that the practice of discussion, writing, and application encourages active participation. These habits mirror the attributes of effective organizations: open communication, shared accountability, and psychological safety. When faculty embody these principles, students mirror them. When leaders model them, teams replicate them.

Faculty who design equitable, interactive classrooms not only raise achievement but rewrite belonging. For historically marginalized students, active learning represents more than a methodology. It is a message: you belong in this conversation. For new or underrepresented employees, participatory leadership conveys the same. Engagement, then, is equity in practice.

———————•••••———————

Leadership Parallel: Engagement isn't contagious by accident. It's transmitted through intentional modeling.

———————•••••———————

Faculty who model curiosity invite inquiry. Leaders who model learning invite innovation. Both create ecosystems where growth is not imposed but inspired.

Reflection: Teaching as Leadership

When we view teaching as leadership, the distinction between education and management fades. Both are acts of stewardship of people, potential, and purpose. The classroom, like the workplace, is a living system that mirrors the energy of its inhabitants.

The most engaged faculty describe teaching not as delivery but as dialogue, not as performance but as partnership. Their influence endures because it transforms mindsets, not just metrics. Likewise, the most effective leaders shape cultures where learning is continuous, curiosity is celebrated, and failing forward is a learning opportunity.

––––––––––– •••••• –––––––––––

From the Classroom to the Boardroom: Teaching and leadership share a common mission to leave people more capable than they were before.

––––––––––– •••••• –––––––––––

Framework for Action: Leading the Learning Culture

1. **Redefine Roles.** See teaching and leadership as overlapping functions both involving coaching, feedback, and vision.

2. **Model Engagement.** Demonstrate curiosity, responsiveness, and vulnerability. Learners mirror what they see.

3. **Design for Interaction.** Build structures that require participation, discussion, reflection, and shared decision-making.

4. **Reward Connection.** Advocate for institutional systems that value mentorship and relational impact alongside output and outcomes.

5. **Invest in Renewal.** Provide faculty and leaders with ongoing professional learning to sustain motivation and creativity.

When teaching becomes leadership, engagement becomes culture. But sustaining that culture requires more than individual effort. It demands institutional alignment.

Chapter 3 explores how systems, policies, and practices can either amplify or erode engagement, and how universities and corporations can design structures that inspire individuals and grow cohesive communities of learners.

When teachers teach with curiosity, students learn with curiosity.
When leaders lead with empathy, teams respond with trust.

CHAPTER 3

The Architecture of Engagement

•◦→⁙←◦•

Redesigning How We Learn and Lead

E very culture of learning begins as a reflection of the people who shape it. In the previous chapter, we explored how faculty and leaders act as catalysts who transform passive environments into communities of curiosity and growth. Yet even the most engaged individual eventually encounters the limits of a system that was not built for adaptability. The next step is architectural: a physical transformation and redesign of the very structures that hold engagement in place.

The study this book is based on yielded rich data and results that inform the insights and suggested interventions throughout the book. The outcomes translate to opportunities to re-envision how we design space and curriculum to promote connectivity and community among disparate groups, whether in a classroom or work environment.

Learning, whether in a classroom or a company, does not happen in isolation. It unfolds within frameworks of policies, traditions, schedules, hierarchies, and technologies that either amplify or suppress human potential. If Chapters 1 and 2 challenged how we think about teaching and leadership, this chapter invites us to rethink the blueprints themselves.

Foundations of Engagement: The Individual as Designer

Engagement begins with the individual, not the institution. It is built from attention, motivation, and purpose, the cognitive and emotional scaffolding that gives structure to learning. Yet self-motivated engagement does not appear spontaneously. It is designed through experience.

The study findings affirmed this truth: when students experienced active learning environments that emphasized participation, feedback, and belonging, their engagement rose significantly, particularly among first-generation, low-income, and underrepresented students. These learners described feeling seen for the first time in an academic space. For them, engagement was not a metric; it was affirmation.

Those same dynamics play out in organizations. Employees who feel invited to contribute meaningfully, are asked for their insights, and trusted to act on them demonstrate higher motivation, creativity, and retention. Engagement is not the product of charisma or compensation; it is a function of inclusion.

––––––––––––––––●●●●●●––––––––––––––––

Teaching Insight: Engagement is not something we deliver to students. It's something we co-design with them.

––––––––––––––––●●●●●●––––––––––––––––

Illustrative Vignette – Higher Education:

A faculty member at a regional university restructures her introductory biology course after noticing high withdrawal rates among first-year students. She shifts from a lecture model to small-group case analyses and reflection journals to increase engagement in the learning process.

Illustrative Vignette – Business:

A manager for a mid-sized firm replaces annual performance reviews with biweekly *learning conversations* with employees. This approach consists of brief check-ins focused on questions and exploration rather than judgments.

Leadership Parallel: Leadership, like teaching, is an intentional choice. Every decision about structure, space, and rhythm either invites or inhibits participation.

Faculty and Leaders as Architects of Experience

At the faculty and leadership level, engagement evolves from personal disposition to professional practice. The study found that faculty who described themselves as "highly engaged" in teaching, and who regularly reflected, experimented, and solicited feedback, tended to create environments where student engagement was more pronounced.

This aligns with what workplace research has shown for years: engagement at the top cascades downward. Teams mirror their leaders' enthusiasm and sense of purpose. When teachers teach with curiosity, students learn with curiosity. When leaders lead with empathy, teams respond with trust.

The central insight here is reciprocity. Engagement is not a one-way flow, but rather it is a loop. In higher education, this means students engage more deeply when they perceive instructors as invested. In business, employees perform better when they perceive their leaders as listeners. The architecture of engagement, then, is not a static moment; it is an ecosystem of relationships.

From the Classroom to the Boardroom: The same relational principles that increase student engagement also enhance workplace culture. Feedback loops, transparency, and shared accountability transform compliance into commitment.

Illustrative Vignette – Business:

A mid-sized marketing firm redesigns its project workflow around collaborative *learning sprints* similar to the agile and lean methodologies. Instead of assigning tasks from the top down, teams identify shared goals, set short learning objectives, and conduct brief reflective debriefs.

When faculty and leaders function as conduits, they don't simply transfer knowledge. They build environments where others can generate it.

Engagement Tip: Design every process around dialogue. The structure of engagement begins with the structure of the conversation.

Systemic Redesign: From Culture to Structure

Personal commitment and engaged teaching can flourish only so far within outdated systems. The study revealed that even the most dedicated faculty often felt constrained by institutional barriers—large class sizes, rigid curricula, and limited professional development. Engagement cannot be sustained in structures that reward output over interaction.

Similarly, in corporate settings, organizational systems built for efficiency often stifle creativity. Employees may be encouraged to "innovate," but without autonomy or support, innovation becomes rhetoric.

To redesign engagement, institutions and organizations must address three distinct layers: culture, policy, and space.

1. **Culture:** Engagement thrives in trust-based environments. Institutions that celebrate experimentation and view mistakes as part of learning create psychological safety.

2. **Policy:** Systems must reward relational work like mentorship, collaboration, and continuous learning. Without structural incentives, engagement remains performative.

3. **Space:** Physical and virtual environments should align with active participation. That means flexible classrooms, collaborative platforms, and hybrid models that balance connection and autonomy.

Teaching Insight: Systems shape behavior. If engagement is the goal, the structure must make engagement the path of least resistance.

Illustrative Vignette – Higher Education:

A large community college district restructures its first-year curriculum into interdisciplinary learning communities. Instead of isolated courses, students move through clusters of subjects with integrated themes and team-taught instruction.

From the Classroom to the Boardroom: One global consulting firm mirrored this approach, replacing its departmental silos with cross-functional "knowledge pods." These pods combined analytics, design, and strategy experts into fluid teams around client challenges. The outcome mirrored the academic study's findings: collaboration produced not just better results, but higher engagement and lower burnout.

The Equity Imperative: Designing for Belonging

Among the most striking outcomes of the study was how active learning pedagogy disproportionately benefited underrepresented students. Students of color, first-generation college-goers, and women in STEM reported higher levels of engagement when learning environments prioritized participation and voice.

Belonging, it turns out, is both a feeling and a function of design. When learning environments shift from hierarchy to inclusion, they distribute confidence as much as knowledge.

For businesses, this lesson is equally urgent. Corporate learning programs that privilege authority over collaboration often perpetuate inequities of voice. By contrast, organizations that practice inclusive facilitation, rotate who leads discussions, and encourage divergent thinking tap into reservoirs of creativity that would otherwise remain silent.

———————•◦•●•◦•———————

Leadership Parallel: Belonging is the foundation of performance. When people feel they belong, they contribute beyond compliance.

———————•◦•●•◦•———————

Illustrative Vignette – Higher Education:

A university in the Midwest redesigns its faculty development model to pair senior professors with early-career colleagues from historically underrepresented backgrounds. The partnership emphasizes mutual mentoring rather than hierarchy and promotes inclusion and engagement.

Reflection: Building Adaptive Systems

The architecture of engagement is never finished. Like any structure, it requires maintenance, renovation, and care. Systems built on past assumptions eventually fail under new pressures. The most successful learning institutions and organizations treat engagement as an evolving infrastructure, not a static ideal.

Redesigning engagement begins with humility, the recognition that systems, however well-intentioned, often serve the convenience of administrators more than the needs of learners. The study underscored this disconnect repeatedly: students thrived when agency, relevance, and interaction were central. Faculty thrived when institutions recognized teaching as both intellectual and relational labor.

In business, the parallel is unmistakable. Engagement improves not through mandates but through meaning, when individuals see how their work contributes to something larger, when leaders listen more than they lecture, and when systems flex to accommodate growth rather than restrict it.

From the Classroom to the Boardroom: The question is no longer whether engagement matters but how we design for it.

Framework for Action: Redesigning the Architecture of Engagement

1. **Map the Experience.** Identify where learners or employees disengage. Whether it is curriculum points, meetings, or workflows, examine what structures contribute to disconnect.

2. **Redefine Success Metrics.** Measure connection, participation, and feedback quality alongside performance and productivity.

3. **Prototype and Pilot.** Test small-scale redesigns like active learning classrooms, hybrid work pods, and peer mentorship models. Use an iterative process based on engagement data.

4. **Align Incentives.** Reward relational and creative contributions equally with quantitative results. Engagement deepens where meaning and recognition align.

5. **Sustain the Culture.** Institutionalize reflection through regular learning audits and dialogue forums that keep engagement visible and actionable.

Every blueprint evolves. If engagement is the architecture of learning and leadership, then culture is the material it's built from. The next chapter turns toward that material and examines how the interplay of values, habits, and shared purpose determines whether the structure endures or erodes.

Teams thrive when leaders design for autonomy rather than control, competence rather than compliance, and belonging rather than hierarchy.

CHAPTER 4

The Architecture of Energy

--------··•➤⥊⬅•··--------

Designing Systems That Inspire Engagement

Chapter 3 explored the scaffolding of engagement, the institutional and organizational systems that either sustain or erode learning. Now we turn our attention inward, toward the energy that powers those systems. The strongest structures are lifeless without movement. What animates them is human motivation, the flow of attention, curiosity, and purpose that transforms design into experience.

In education and in business alike, the most innovative spaces are those that are dynamic and energized. Their spaces hum with energy because they have been designed not only for efficiency, but for engagement. This chapter examines the inner architecture of that energy: how motivation forms the foundation, how mindfulness and meaning shape the design, and how participation expresses the outcome.

Motivation as Foundation

Every structure begins with a foundation, and in learning environments, that foundation is motivation. The study revealed that engagement is strongest when the three psychological needs of autonomy, competence, and relatedness are fulfilled. Together, they form what Deci and Ryan (1985) called self-determination theory.

When students experience autonomy, they perceive agency over their learning; when they experience competence, they believe they can succeed; and when they experience relatedness, they feel connected to others in the environment. These conditions aren't "soft" factors, but they are the load-bearing pillars of motivation, and when intentionally designed, they create a structure resilient enough to support sustained engagement.

Teaching Insight: Building motivation is intentional. Structure the classroom and the organization to meet human needs before focusing on human outcomes.

Faculty who built autonomy into their courses, allowing students to choose project topics or problem-solving approaches, reported higher engagement and persistence. For underprepared students, that choice carried symbolic weight; it said, "Your voice matters." Similarly, when instructors scaffolded competence through formative feedback and relational teaching, students described a greater sense of confidence and capability.

In business, this same principle applies. Teams thrive when leaders design for autonomy rather than control, competence rather than compliance, and belonging rather than hierarchy.

Leadership Parallel: The most effective leaders are architects of motivation. They design systems that grant people ownership, reinforce capability, and build connection.

Illustrative Vignette – Business:

The leadership of a financial services firm redesigns its analyst performance management system to emphasize self-directed goal setting and peer mentoring. This approach builds trust, promotes productivity, and increases engagement.

This echoes what we see in education: self-determined motivation internalizes accountability. Whether students or employees, people invest more deeply when the structure honors their autonomy, builds their skill, creates teachable moments, and affirms their belonging.

From the Classroom to the Boardroom: Both students and employees disengage when environments communicate control and exclusion. The dynamic of motivation, by contrast, communicates invitation: You can do it. You belong. You matter.

Mindfulness and Meaning as Design Elements

If motivation forms the foundation, mindfulness and meaning are the design elements that give a structure integrity and character. They determine not only how energy flows through a system, but how it feels to participate in it.

The study found that students who practiced mindfulness techniques, such as staying present, reflecting deeply, and remaining open to multiple perspectives, experienced higher engagement and conceptual understanding. Langer (1997) defined mindfulness as the simple act of noticing, but its implications are profound. When students are encouraged to notice distinctions, challenge assumptions, and entertain new interpretations, they begin to see learning not as memorization, but as creation.

This principle extends directly to business innovation. Organizations that cultivate mindfulness do not simply train employees to react, but train them to notice. Noticing patterns, tensions, or opportunities allows teams to innovate rather than repeat. It is the same mental agility that underpins creative problem-solving and adaptive leadership.

———————— •••••• ————————

Engagement Tip: Design for awareness, not automation. Systems that allow reflection produce insight. Systems that demand speed more often produce error.

———————— •••••• ————————

Illustrative Vignette – Higher Education:

An instructor integrates *pause points* into lectures consisting of two-minute intervals that allow students to reflect on what surprised or confused them. These micro-moments became structural beams allowing students to process complexity rather than passively record information.

In corporate terms, *pause points* mirror *root cause analysis* or *learning sprints* which are intentional pauses to ask what worked, what didn't, and why.

Illustrative Vignette – Business:

A global tech firm's teams practice the discipline of conducting *root cause analysis* or *learning sprints* for each project to assess outcomes and improve processes.

The common thread: engagement grows through reflection.

––––––––––––––––—•••◆•◆•••—––––––––––––––––

Leadership Parallel: Mindful leadership builds adaptive cultures. When reflection becomes an integrated design feature rather than an afterthought, learning becomes continuous.

––––––––––––––––—•••◆•◆•••—––––––––––––––––

Meaning amplifies mindfulness. When people understand why their work or study matters, they invest more energy in how they do it. The study revealed that when faculty explicitly connected course material to students' goals, values, or communities, engagement deepened significantly. Students who once viewed assignments as chores began describing them as challenges.

In business, meaning and purpose function as a strategic anchor. Simon Sinek's (2009) principle, "Start with Why," translates directly to self-determination theory. It emphasizes the importance of understanding and articulating purpose, which aligns with self-determination theory's focus on autonomy, competence, and relatedness. Leaders who articulate why a project matters, and who connect tasks to larger organizational impact, help employees move from compliance to commitment. In other words, intrinsic motivation thrives on purpose.

———————•••••———————

From the Classroom to the Boardroom: Meaning turns activity into contribution. When people see their role in the larger design, motivation becomes momentum.

———————•••••———————

At a community college, an environmental science course embedded local sustainability projects into the curriculum. Students collected data on water quality and presented their findings to city officials. Grades improved as did sense of belonging. Students began calling themselves scientists, not students.

———————•••••———————

Teaching Insight: Make relevance visible. Engagement increases when learners and workers see how today's effort connects to tomorrow's impact.

———————•••••———————

In a similar way, a consumer-goods company launched "micro-missions," enabling employees to volunteer small amounts of time for environmental or community initiatives aligned with company goals. Engagement rose across departments not because of monetary incentives, but because of meaning.

Mindfulness and meaning are thus the design elements that hold a culture of learning together. They ensure that the architecture of energy remains flexible, responsive, and human-centered.

Participation as Expression of Energy

If motivation provides the foundation and mindfulness shapes the design, participation is the living expression of that intersection, the moment when structure meets movement and engagement becomes visible.

Astin (1999) described this as the physical and psychological energy that students devote to learning. In classrooms and workplaces alike, participation is the behavioral echo of intrinsic motivation. It is how we know a structure is working.

The study found that when students were invited to co-create knowledge through collaborative projects, discussions, or peer instruction, they not only learned more, their sense of belonging increased. Participation closed the distance between teacher and learner, turning passive observation into active engagement.

———————•••••———————

Teaching Insight: Participation is the heartbeat of engagement. Design experiences that require contribution, not just attendance.

———————•••••———————

Illustrative Vignette – Higher Education:

An introductory business course integrates a community-based event driven by the students into the curriculum. Students partner with local businesses, solicit sponsors, develop a marketing campaign, oversee the budget, and track metrics for success.

Illustrative Vignette – Business:

A global consulting firm implements cross-functional *design pods* that allow employees at all levels to co-develop solutions. The approach is designed to spur faster problem-solving and build stronger collaboration across departments.

———————•◦●◦•———————

Leadership Parallel: Engagement thrives where contribution is expected and valued. Ownership is designed into the system.

———————•◦●◦•———————

Participation is also an equity tool. The study confirmed that underrepresented and first-generation students benefitted most from environments that encouraged active contribution. For these students, participation was more than involvement; it was validation. In organizations, employees from marginalized backgrounds report similar effects. When leadership actively structures participation, such as rotating meeting facilitation, and seeking diverse perspectives, engagement gaps narrow.

———————•◦●◦•———————

From the Classroom to the Boardroom: Design participation into the system. Diversity of voice matters when it shapes decisions.

———————•◦●◦•———————

Carini, Kuh, and Klein (2006) demonstrated that students in active learning environments showed gains not only in academic achievement but in confidence and interpersonal skills. Likewise, teams that collaborate actively report stronger trust and innovation outcomes.

To design for participation, educators and leaders can:

- Create low-barrier entry points for contribution (quick polls, peer checks, breakout discussions).
- Diversify modes of participation (verbal, written, visual, collaborative).
- Reward risk-taking and reflection as much as results.

———————••●◆●••———————

Engagement Tip: Redefine participation. Presence is not engagement; contribution is.

———————••●◆●••———————

In essence, participation is the visible architecture of energy and how systems display life. Classrooms and companies that pulse with dialogue, experimentation, and feedback are not chaotic; they are robust.

Reflection: Sustaining the Architecture

Engagement doesn't emerge spontaneously; it's designed and maintained. Across both education and business, the study underscores that motivation, mindfulness, and participation are not separate strategies but interlocking structures within one architecture of energy.

For educators, the implication is clear: design courses around autonomy, reflection, and contribution. For leaders, the message is identical: design cultures around ownership, awareness, and collaboration.

———————••●◆●••———————

Leadership Parallel: Sustainable engagement is structural integrity. Systems endure when their design aligns with human nature.

———————••●◆●••———————

The classroom that invites dialogue mirrors the meeting that encourages dissent. The professor who links theory to lived experience parallels the executive who connects strategy to purpose. In both spaces, engagement is engineered by design.

Framework for Action: Designing Systems That Inspire Energy

1. **Build Autonomy Into Structure.** Design roles, projects, and courses that provide choice within clear boundaries.

2. **Make Reflection Routine.** Incorporate moments of mindfulness, such as debriefs, journaling, and retrospectives, into every workflow.

3. **Anchor Work in Meaning.** Connect individual tasks to shared goals and societal impact.

4. **Design for Contribution.** Build platforms where multiple voices shape the outcome.

5. **Audit the Architecture.** Regularly assess whether systems invite or inhibit engagement and redesign accordingly.

The architecture of energy reminds us that engagement is neither accidental nor ephemeral; it is the result of intentional design. By aligning motivation, mindfulness, and participation, educators and leaders create systems that convert human potential into collective momentum.

Where Chapter 4 explored the energy that fuels learning, Chapter 5 shows how that energy is channeled into motion. In the next chapter, we'll move from principles to practice, exploring active learning pedagogy as the actionable blueprint that operationalizes this architecture in classrooms and organizations alike.

CHAPTER 5

From Passive to Powerful

―――――・◦→✳←◦・――――――

Designing Learning and Leadership That Engage Minds and Move People

In the previous chapter, we examined the architecture of energy and how motivation, mindfulness, and participation create the conditions for engagement to flourish. But architecture alone cannot animate a system. Design gives us the blueprint; activation brings it to life. This chapter explores how educators and leaders alike can move from structure to spark, and from systems that allow engagement to those that ignite it.

The bridge between teaching and leadership has never been clearer. In both domains, the challenge is not the absence of information, but the presence of inertia. Engagement requires more than content; it demands design that moves people intellectually, emotionally, and collectively. Active learning pedagogy offers that design, a framework that transforms passivity into participation and instruction into inspiration.

The Theory Behind Engagement

Active learning begins with a shift in philosophy and a reframing of what it means to teach, to lead, and to learn. It rejects the assumption that knowledge is best transmitted through one-way communication. Instead, it aligns with the same principles that drive modern leadership: participation, collaboration, and meaning-making.

At its core, active learning is grounded in social constructivism, the belief that knowledge is co-created through interaction and experience rather than delivered intact from one mind to another. This theory, advanced by John Dewey, Jean Piaget, and Lev Vygotsky, revolutionized how educators and leaders understand growth. It positioned learning as relational, dynamic, and fundamentally social.

Dewey (1922) saw learning as inquiry, an iterative process of questioning, testing, and reflecting. For him, classrooms should resemble laboratories of thought, not lecture halls of compliance. Piaget (1964) focused on cognitive development, showing that learners construct understanding by integrating new information with prior experience. Vygotsky (1978) extended this further, arguing that development happens in relationship with peers, mentors, and culture. His concept of the zone of proximal development (ZPD) captures this essence: people learn best when supported just beyond their current ability, through guidance and collaboration.

Teaching Insight: Learning begins at the edge of comfort. The role of the instructor or leader is to design the bridge between what is known and what is possible.

These ideas extend far beyond education. In business, they underpin the shift from command-and-control management to collaborative, purpose-driven leadership. A manager operating in the spirit of Vygotsky designs opportunities for growth that include stretch assignments, coaching, and team problem-solving that function as modern-day zones of proximal development.

———————•••••———————

Leadership Parallel: Leaders are facilitators of discovery. They don't just direct but they also design environments where people learn through doing and reflecting.

———————•••••———————

Illustrative Vignette – Higher Education:

A political science professor redesigns her course on international relations using a *policy lab* model. Instead of lectures, students form small research teams advising a simulated foreign ministry. With guidance, they negotiate trade deals, draft policy memos, and present to mock ambassadors.

Illustrative Vignette – Business:

A global manufacturing company adopts a *learning sprint* model for leadership development. Participants tackle business challenges in teams, alternating between short content sessions and collaborative problem-solving. Rather than passively absorbing theories, leaders apply them immediately, learning from feedback through an iterative process.

From the Classroom to the Boardroom: Active learning reframes both teaching and leadership as acts of facilitation. The most effective environments, whether academic or corporate, design for participation, reflection, and growth.

Designing for Active Learning

Theory without design remains abstract. The power of active learning lies in how it is built and how structure, space, and strategy come together to make engagement inevitable rather than optional.

Active learning design follows five principles, all of which apply equally to classrooms and organizations:

1. **Center the Learner.** Move from information delivery to inquiry. Design experiences where participants shape outcomes through questioning, problem-solving, and reflection.

2. **Activate Cognition.** Prioritize thinking over doing. Activities must engage analysis, synthesis, and evaluation not just movement or discussion.

3. **Build Collaboration.** Design for interdependence. The group, not the individual, becomes the primary site of learning.

4. **Embed Feedback.** Construct feedback loops that are immediate, iterative, and constructive.

5. **Create Relevance.** Connect learning directly to real-world purpose and application.

———————••●●••———————

Engagement Tip: Design backward. Start with the experience you want people to have, then design content, structure, and feedback to achieve it.

———————••●●••———————

In higher education, these design principles transform classrooms from static spaces into dynamic ecosystems of inquiry. Faculty may replace lectures with case studies where students solve real-world challenges, or an instructor might host small group discussions that blend academic analysis with creative response.

In organizations, the same architecture applies. Leadership teams use project-based learning to engage employees in solving business challenges. Sales departments run role-playing simulations to refine negotiation skills. Even performance reviews are being reimagined as iterative, two-way dialogues that focus on development rather than judgment.

Illustrative Vignette – Higher Education:

At a large public university, a biology department implements *flipped classrooms*, assigning lectures as video homework and dedicating class time to collaborative problem-solving.

Illustrative Vignette – Business:

A healthcare organization shifts from lecture to dialogue during staff training. Instead of mandatory compliance sessions, employees participated in interactive case discussions about ethical decision-making.

Leadership Parallel: Good design democratizes learning. It transforms passive audiences into active architects of knowledge.

Putting Pedagogy into Practice

Active learning succeeds when design meets execution and when spaces are animated by facilitation. The instructor or leader becomes a conductor, orchestrating collaboration, curiosity, and reflection.

Bonwell and Eison (1991) defined active learning as "students doing things and thinking about what they are doing." The dual emphasis on doing and thinking captures its essence: activity without reflection is devoid of meaning; reflection without activity is inertia. The magic lies in their interplay.

Teaching Insight: Engagement happens at the intersection of effort and insight.

This principle also drives modern team leadership. The most effective organizations blend action and reflection through the agile practices of brief cycles of planning, doing, reviewing, and adapting. These loops mirror the structure of active learning: iterative, participatory, and evidence-based.

Illustrative Vignette – Higher Education:

A nursing instructor redesigns clinical labs into micro-simulations, where students practice rapid decision-making under time constraints. Each scenario is followed by guided debriefs linking theory to practice.

Illustrative Vignette – Business:

A logistics firm introduces debriefs after each major project completion. Teams spend fifteen minutes discussing what worked, what failed, and what was learned. The practice improves delivery efficiency and strengthens cross-team collaboration.

From the Classroom to the Boardroom: Reflection is the hinge between experience and growth. Whether in a lab or a boardroom, engagement deepens when people pause to make meaning together.

Active learning also depends on psychological safety, a concept widely discussed in organizational psychology and equally vital in education. Students, like employees, need to know they can speak, experiment, and fail without ridicule. Faculty who establish inclusive norms, such as inviting every voice and honoring multiple perspectives, create conditions where curiosity thrives.

In business, Amy Edmondson's research on psychological safety shows that teams who feel safe to ask questions and admit mistakes outperform those who do not. The same holds in classrooms: learning stagnates where fear dominates.

———— •◦●◦●◦• ————

Leadership Parallel: Safety fuels risk-taking. When people feel secure, they innovate; when they fear failure, they comply.

———— •◦●◦●◦• ————

From Classroom to Culture

The true measure of active learning isn't what happens in the classroom. It's what happens afterward. The goal is transfer: the ability to apply learning across contexts, disciplines, and challenges.

In higher education, transfer shows up when students connect classroom insights to internships, research projects, and civic engagement. In business, it manifests as innovation, collaboration, and continuous improvement.

———— •◦●◦●◦• ————

Teaching Insight: Active learning is culture-building not just a means to teach content. It teaches us how to learn, how to collaborate, and how to adapt.

———— •◦●◦●◦• ————

Illustrative Vignette – Higher Education:

A communications course requires students to partner with local nonprofits to develop messaging campaigns. Students participate in the application of communication theory to real-world community problems.

Illustrative Vignette – Business:

A global software company restructures its leadership program around "action learning projects" that addresses live business issues. Teams implement solutions while learning strategy, design thinking, and collaboration. The result is skill development and business innovation.

———————•••◆•••———————

Engagement Tip: End every learning experience with a bridge. Ask participants: "Where will you use this next?"

———————•••◆•••———————

Active learning, in this sense, is both pedagogy and philosophy. It's a way of designing environments that cultivate curiosity, autonomy, and meaning. It teaches not *what* to think, but *how* to keep thinking.

———————•••◆•••———————

From the Classroom to the Boardroom: When organizations adopt active learning principles, they become learning organizations capable of continuous reinvention.

———————•••◆•••———————

Reflection: Designing for Momentum

Active learning isn't about activity; it's about agency. It shifts learning from passive absorption to purposeful engagement which is just as vital in the workplace as in higher education. Faculty who adopt it rediscover their joy in teaching. Leaders who emulate it rediscover their teams' capacity to learn, adapt, and thrive.

———————•••◆•••———————

Leadership Parallel: The classroom and corporations share the same blueprint: design for curiosity, build for collaboration, and measure by growth.

———————•••◆•••———————

Framework for Action: Activating Learning and Leadership

1. **Start with Purpose.** Define what engagement should accomplish and design backward.

2. **Facilitate, Don't Dictate.** Replace command with coaching, lectures with dialogue, and performance metrics with learning outcomes.

3. **Structure Reflection.** Embed debriefs and feedback loops in every process.

4. **Model Inclusion.** Ensure multiple voices have space and weight in discussion and decision-making.

5. **Sustain the Culture.** Treat learning as a living system that reviews, refines, and redesigns continuously.

Active learning transforms instruction into knowledge and it operationalizes systems. But this transformation doesn't happen in empty space. The next chapter explores the environments that spur this momentum: how physical, digital, and cultural spaces influence engagement, participation, and connection. If active learning is the catalyst, space is the converter. Together, they determine how far and how powerfully learning can go.

CHAPTER 6

The Space Between Learning and Doing

·⸱•⸱➤⸱✳⸱⸱•⸱·

Why Physical Environments Matter More Than We Think

The energy of engagement, once sparked through active learning, must have somewhere to live. Ideas, after all, are shaped as much by their surroundings as by their source. The previous chapter explored how learning and leadership become powerful when people are invited to participate fully, to think, create, and collaborate. But even the most dynamic pedagogy can falter in an environment that resists movement. Now our attention turns to the physical, digital, and cultural spaces that either amplify or extinguish the spark of engagement. Here, we explore how design becomes the silent teacher and how every wall, table, and layout tells a story about who belongs and how learning unfolds.

From Pews to Pods: A Brief History of Learning Spaces

If the modern boardroom looks suspiciously like a lecture hall, that is because both share ancestry with ancient amphitheaters. When the Greeks carved semicircular tiers into stone, they created not just an architectural marvel but a social hierarchy: a stage for the speaker and steps for the listeners. The design made perfect sense for an oral tradition when knowledge lived in the voice, not on the page, but it also established a lasting symbol of power. The few spoke. The many listened.

Centuries later, the Roman Catholic Church perfected the model. As Pope Gregory VII standardized clerical education, vast auditoria became centers of instruction, with lecturers dictating sacred texts to scribes. These early classrooms prioritized reach over interaction. The goal was efficient dissemination, not dialogue. By the time American higher education began shaping its own campuses, the design template was already set: front-facing rows, fixed seating, and a focal podium.

Even as the Industrial Revolution re-engineered the world outside, the classroom stayed curiously static. Desks aligned like factory lines. Efficiency trumped engagement. The implicit lesson was obedience: sit, face forward, absorb. The physical environment mirrored the management philosophies of the era, hierarchical, compartmentalized, and orderly.

But the 21st-century learner no longer fits the 19th-century room. Collaboration has replaced command. Ideas move fast. The question today is not whether learning happens, but whether the environment helps or hinders it.

Leadership Insight: The space you inherit communicates your culture long before you do. Rows suggest control; circles suggest conversation. The geometry of the room teaches as powerfully as the curriculum itself.

The Architecture of Attention

Environmental psychologists like Roger Barker (1965) argued decades ago that behavior settings and physical contexts with social norms directly influence how people act. Yet only recently have organizations begun to treat the classroom, the training room, and the workspace as behavioral technology. Every design choice, whether it be lighting, temperature, color, sightlines, or acoustics, affects cognitive load and emotional tone (Hill and Epps, 2010; Uline et al., 2010).

A well-lit room with adjustable furniture does not simply look modern; it allows movement, signals autonomy, and lowers hierarchy. Air quality influences focus. Poor acoustics erode collaboration as quickly as bad leadership. Design, in other words, is not just about aesthetics. It is about strategy.

When educators at North Carolina State launched the Student-Centered Active Learning Environment with Upside-Down Pedagogies (SCALE-UP) initiative (Beichner, 2014), they were not just swapping chairs; they were rewriting behavior. Round tables replaced rows, erasing the front of the room. Screens and whiteboards encircled the space, allowing students to look and think in every direction. The result? Higher conceptual understanding and lower failure rates, particularly among women and first-generation students.

MIT's Technology Enabled Active Learning (TEAL) classroom model (Dori and Belcher, 2005) reached similar conclusions: when learners face one another, they engage one another. The University of Minnesota's Active Learning Center (ALC) and Iowa's Transform, Interact, Learn, Engage (TILE) initiative extended that philosophy, coupling technology with flexible room layouts. Across these experiments, one constant emerged: space design and pedagogy co-evolve. You cannot modernize one and ignore the other.

---•••••---

Design Tip: When reconfiguring any campus or corporate learning space, start by removing the concept of "front." Wherever people face each other, proximity enhances learning.

---•••••---

What Classrooms Teach Corporate America

Corporate leaders often spend millions on training programs while hosting them in windowless rooms designed for compliance testing. Yet the research from higher education translates directly. The same principles that make students curious make employees creative.

Consider Deloitte University (DU) campuses across the globe in Texas, Canada, Mexico, Belgium, India, and Singapore. The design of the campuses is consistent with active learning theory and the physical environment in which it can thrive: leadership and learning centers, reconfigurable spaces, multipurpose training rooms, and spaces that invite collaboration through chance meetings. Participants can move from plenary discussions to breakout pods with the rhythm of a workshop, not a lecture. Teams of thought leaders, professionals, and client groups are immersed in engaged learning and growth at DU.

IDEO's global studios apply similar logic. Maker spaces, breakout areas, accessible workshops, and social spaces, desks on casters, walls that double as whiteboards, and integrated furniture and technology help teams access and share information seamlessly. At IDEO's studios, teams routinely reconfigure the environment to match the project phase. The philosophy is simple: space should invite the behavior you want. If you want experimentation, design for flexibility. If you want reflection, design for quiet zones.

Even tech giants like Google use the classroom metaphor inversely by turning the office into a learning ecosystem. Informal huddle rooms, nooks, and open floor plates provide spontaneous learning moments among employees that reinforce "each one, teach one."

———————•◦●◦•———————

From the Classroom to the Boardroom: Active learning isn't an educational fad; it's a management practice. The same conditions that drive student engagement, like autonomy, social connection, and feedback, also fuel innovation and retention in the workplace.

———————•◦●◦•———————

The Design Psychology of Engagement

Engagement is as emotional as it is intellectual. The environment cues safety, belonging, and status which are all prerequisites for risk-taking and creativity. Self-determination theory reminds us that people thrive when autonomy, competence, and relatedness are met. Physical design can nurture or negate each of these.

- **Autonomy:** Movable furniture, writable surfaces, and access to technology signal trust. They allow learners to own the space.

- **Competence:** Clear sightlines, quality acoustics, and accessible resources reduce frustration, supporting mastery.

- **Relatedness:** Circular layouts and shared surfaces foster eye contact, proximity to one another, and dialogue, deepening connection.

Corporate spaces often default to aesthetics before psychology. A sleek boardroom may photograph well but perform poorly if the table is too long for natural conversation. Likewise, the popular open-office plan can stifle focus if privacy zones are absent. The goal is not openness for its own sake, but *purposeful permeability:* enough connection to spark exchange, enough boundary to support thought.

―――――――――― ••◗◖•• ――――――――――

Leadership Insight: Design is a form of inclusive leadership. The chair you choose tells people whether their voice matters.

―――――――――― ••◗◖•• ――――――――――

Building the Modern Learning Ecosystem

What makes an environment truly engaging? Across universities and corporations, five design dimensions consistently appear.

1. Flexibility

Spaces should morph to match the learning mode which moves from discussion, presentation, and reflection to collaboration. Movable furniture, mobile power, and modular technology support constant adaptation.

2. Visibility

Engagement requires sightlines both literal and social. Everyone should see the speaker, the screen, and one another. Transparency of design mirrors transparent dialogue.

3. Accessibility

Technology and tools must be easy to reach and intuitive to use. Complexity with no purpose kills implementation and participation.

4. Comfort

Temperature, acoustics, and ergonomics matter. A space that supports physical comfort frees cognitive bandwidth.

5. Identity

Spaces communicate values. Art, color, and materiality should reflect the organization's purpose and diversity. When people see themselves in the environment, they engage more fully.

——————●●◆●●——————

Design Framework: The Five Dimensions of an Engaging Space
These principles are not a checklist but an ecosystem. Adjust one,
and the others respond.

——————●●◆●●——————

When Walls Start to Move

The future of learning environments, both academic and corporate, may look less like rooms and more like networks. Pop-up classrooms, hybrid studios, and virtual collaborative platforms blur the boundary between physical and digital. Yet even in virtual space, design thinking still applies. Camera angles, lighting, background, and screen layout create psychological space. The challenge for leaders and designers is to think spatially about interaction, regardless of medium.

MIT's TEAL/Studio Physics Project, for instance, integrates students into the discussion by using multiple projectors classroom-wide to display images around the room so everyone can see and participate. The installation of whiteboards on all walls, ceiling-mounted cameras, and laptop connections at faculty and student stations further promotes an interactive learning environment. Similarly, forward-thinking companies use technology and design to preserve spatial equity and promote dialogue among teams.

--------------------•◦●◆●◦•--------------------

Leadership Insight: Hybrid is not a compromise; it's an opportunity to design inclusivity into engagement.

--------------------•◦●◆●◦•--------------------

Reflection: The Human Geometry of Learning

In the end, the most sophisticated environment cannot compensate for poor leadership or uninspired pedagogy. But when behavior and space align, the effect is exponential. The room becomes a silent coach, reminding us that mental, social, and physical learning can be reimagined.

A classroom, a boardroom, a studio: all are stages for human growth. The design question is deceptively simple: Does this place invite participation or inhibit it?

If Chapter 5 explored the psychology of active learning, this chapter reveals its physical capabilities. Behavior is energy; environment is its container. When leaders, educators, and designers collaborate, the container expands, and so does potential.

Framework for Action: Designing for Engagement

1. **Start with Purpose.** Define what engagement looks like before sketching the space plan.

2. **Prototype the Space.** Rearrange furniture for a week and observe behavioral change. Iterate before investing.

3. **Measure Behavior, Not Beauty.** Survey movement, interaction, and feedback frequency, not décor approval.

4. **Train the Facilitators.** A flexible room still needs an agile instructor or leader.

5. **Sustain the Culture.** Physical change sparks momentum; policy and practice sustain it.

Engaged environments remind us that learning is not confined to instruction. It's embedded in architecture, culture, and everyday experience. The space between learning and doing is, quite literally, the space we design.

In classrooms and organizations alike, engagement is rarely a problem of knowledge or skill. It is a problem of connection between people, values, and purpose.

CHAPTER 7

Beyond the Data

---•※•---

Translating Insight Into Impact

The previous chapter explored how physical and digital environments shape the energy of engagement and how space itself can invite curiosity, collaboration, and creativity. Yet even the most dynamic spaces fall silent without one essential element: connection. The architecture of engagement is not complete until people inhabit it meaningfully. Shifts from structure to relationship are a function of examining how human connection transforms data and systems into belonging and engagement that permeate culture.

In classrooms and organizations alike, engagement is rarely a problem of knowledge or skill. It is a problem of connection between people, values, and purpose. What happens when educators and leaders intentionally design for that connection? What emerges when relationships become the foundation rather than the byproduct of learning and leadership?

From Insight to Understanding

The study's outcomes made one truth clear: engagement is fundamentally relational. Faculty who cultivated authentic relationships with students consistently saw higher levels of motivation, persistence, and achievement. Likewise, leaders who invested time and trust in their teams observed deeper commitment and innovation. Data revealed what intuition already knew: human beings learn, grow, and perform best in environments where they feel seen, valued, and connected.

In higher education, these relationships often began with small acts: knowing a student's name, offering flexible office hours, or integrating reflective assignments that allow students to share personal perspectives. Faculty who described themselves as "engaged with their students" were more likely to design courses emphasizing collaboration, feedback, and real-world application. Their students reported feeling "invited into the conversation," not "talked at."

In business, the pattern mirrors this precisely. Engagement metrics improve most where leaders practice relational awareness, creating psychological safety, celebrating contribution, and providing meaningful feedback. The numbers may differ, but the principle is universal: relationships drive results.

Teaching Insight: Data may measure performance, but relationships create it.

Illustrative Vignette – Faculty:

A first-year writing professor redesigns her course to include individual one-to-one conferences, replacing a portion of lecture time with personalized feedback sessions.

Illustrative Vignette – Business:

A regional sales manager introduces weekly "lunch and learns" for her distributed team. The agenda: open conversation about wins, challenges, and lessons learned.

Leadership Parallel: Relational engagement is strategic engagement. Leaders who invest in people's sense of belonging build loyalty that no incentive program can replicate.

From Understanding to Action

Understanding engagement as relational requires redesigning best practices around connection. The most effective faculty and leaders did not simply care about relationships; they engineered them through intentional structures that reinforce trust, participation, and shared purpose.

In education, this often means reshaping how success is defined. Faculty in the study who prioritized dialogue over delivery and co-creation over control saw profound differences in student behavior. Their classrooms became communities of practice rather than spaces of performance. Students spoke more, collaborated more, and, most importantly, believed more in their own self-efficacy to learn.

Similarly, in business, engagement flourishes when leaders replace authority with agency. Organizations that embed relational design through mentorship programs, collaborative planning, and feedback rituals turn teams into networks of learning. Engagement stops being an initiative and becomes a habit.

Engagement Tip: Design rituals of connection. Regular check-ins, collaborative meetings, and shared reflection moments transform relationships into meaningful growth opportunities.

Illustrative Vignette – Faculty:

A psychology professor launches "Mindful Mondays," starting each class with a brief conversation about stress, focus, or gratitude. The practice takes five minutes but can reshape the tone of the class and semester.

Illustrative Vignette – Business:

A global design firm institutes "Morning Huddles", ten-minute morning gatherings where employees share current priorities and one personal highlight. Over time, these micro-interactions can strengthen cross-departmental collaboration and reduce friction between teams.

From the Classroom to the Boardroom: Connection doesn't require complexity. It requires consistency. The strongest organizations and classrooms are those where people expect to engage with one another, not just with tasks.

Understanding becomes action when engagement is embedded in systems. When relationship-centered practices, like open dialogue, mentorship, and shared reflection, are designed into schedules, spaces, and strategies, belonging becomes operationalized.

From Action to Culture

Action repeated over time becomes part of the culture. What begins as individual effort What begins with one professor's feedback conference or one leader's listening session can evolve into an organizational identity grounded in belonging. The study found that when engagement practices were institutionally supported, their effects multiplied. Faculty in relationally driven departments described greater satisfaction, collaboration, and innovation. Students noticed too. The difference was palpable: classrooms felt "alive."

In business, these same dynamics distinguish high-performing organizations. Gallup's long-standing research on engagement shows that cultures emphasizing strengths, trust, and dialogue outperform peers in productivity and profitability. But the relational architecture behind those outcomes is often invisible and embedded in how leaders model vulnerability, invite input, and distribute ownership.

———————•●◆●••———————

Teaching Insight: Culture grows where connection is fostered, not mandated.

———————•●◆●••———————

Illustrative Vignette – Faculty:

At a liberal arts college, an interdisciplinary teaching team develops a "learning community" model that links three first-year courses around shared themes. Faculty co-teach, share assessment strategies, and meet weekly to reflect on student progress. The goal: higher retention, deeper faculty engagement, and a campus-wide conversation about collaborative teaching.

Illustrative Vignette – Business:

A mid-sized technology company built its culture around peer-led innovation. Every quarter, employees host "Idea Labs," pitching small-scale experiments to improve processes or products. Leadership attended but did not dominate. The initiative cultivates a shared sense of ownership and creativity.

―――――――――•••――――――――

Leadership Parallel: Leadership is culture in motion. The behaviors leaders model, like curiosity, empathy, and collaboration, set the rhythm that others follow.

―――――――――•••――――――――

Culture, once established, reinforces itself. Faculty who feel supported are more likely to invest in student relationships. Employees who feel trusted are more likely to take initiative. The architecture of engagement becomes self-sustaining when connection moves from individual intention to collective identity.

From Culture to Legacy

Every system, academic or corporate, leaves a legacy not just in what it achieves, but in how it treats people along the way. The enduring outcome of this study is the recognition that relationships are not ancillary to learning and leadership; they are central.

Faculty engagement matters because it shapes the ecosystem of the learning experience. Students who experience authentic connection with instructors carry that confidence into their professional lives. Likewise, employees who feel seen and supported by leaders become mentors, innovators, and culture builders themselves. The ripple of relational design extends far beyond the classroom or conference room. It influences how people see themselves as capable of shaping the environments they inhabit.

From the Classroom to the Boardroom: Relational design creates legacy through people. The lessons we teach and the values we model echo in every space our learners and teams eventually lead.

Illustrative Vignette – Faculty and Leadership:

In a university-business partnership, faculty and corporate mentors co-develop a capstone leadership program where students work on real consulting projects. The collaboration blurs the lines between academia and enterprise, modeling relational leadership in action.

The legacy of engagement, then, is human architecture and the networks of trust, empathy, and shared purpose that outlast any single system or structure.

Reflection: Designing Relationships That Last

Relationships are the quiet infrastructure of engagement. They hold the weight of learning and leadership alike. The study affirmed what great educators and great leaders have always known: data can inform practice, but only relationships transform it.

Engagement doesn't emerge from metrics, policies, or programs; it grows from presence, empathy, and shared purpose. When we design systems that honor those principles, we build not just effective institutions or profitable companies, we build communities of meaning.

———————•●◆●•———————

Leadership Parallel: Relationships are renewable energy. When designed with care, they power learning, growth, and innovation long after the initial spark fades.

———————•●◆●•———————

Framework for Action: Building Relational Architecture

1. **Listen Intentionally.** Create structures for dialogue that go beyond evaluation. Regular check-ins, reflection circles, or mentoring sessions are proven tactics.

2. **Model Empathy.** Demonstrate curiosity about people's experiences before judging their outcomes.

3. **Connect Purpose to Practice.** Link every task or lesson to shared values and long-term goals.

4. **Empower Collaboration.** Design opportunities for co-creation across boundaries whether its students with faculty or teams with leadership.

5. **Sustain Through Story.** Celebrate and share relational successes. Stories transmit culture faster than policy.

Looking Ahead

The architecture of engagement is never finished. Each connection made, each culture shaped, extends the blueprint further. The future of learning and leadership depends not on new technologies or management theories, but on how we continue to design for belonging, purpose, and trust.

What we build through relationships today becomes the legacy others inherit tomorrow.

---●◆●---

Relationships are the quiet infrastructure of engagement. They hold the weight of learning and leadership alike.

---●◆●---

Acknowledgments

───────•◦❋◦•───────

Pursuing a doctoral degree was not on my radar. I was completing an MBA and thought that would be my final degree. Then I had a conversation with the dean of the business school who would change my way of thinking. The dean hired me to adjunct lecture a marketing class upon graduation from the MBA program. It was a class I taught while having a full-time job outside of academia. After the class was complete, she talked with me about considering a doctoral program and offered advice on how I could get started and even obtain funding. At the time, it was not a burning desire for me, but my interest was sparked with that one conversation. Starting a doctoral program to earn a Ph.D. led me to the research on active learning and engagement that is the basis for this book.

I want to express my appreciation for the support of family and friends. My parents have always encouraged me and my sisters to keep learning, and we have. I am also indebted to architecture, engineering, and construction (A/E/C) industry colleagues who have encouraged my journey.

My ability to be a scholarly practitioner and use what I have learned is due to the many clients, A/E/C industry organizations, and employers I have worked and volunteered with and their willingness to let me experiment, try something new, and bring insight from a new space to the discussion. Engaging students can set the scene for learning opportunities that promote significant cognitive, behavioral, and emotional growth in the near term and build the foundation for engaged employees in the future.

References And Resources

ACT Education Corp (2025). *The ACT Profile Report National – Graduating Class 2024.* Retrieved from: https://www.act.org/content/dam/act/unsecured/documents/2024-act-national-graduating-class-profile-report.pdf

Altbach, P. G., Gumport, P. J., & Berdahl, R. O. (Eds.). (2011). *American higher education in the twenty-first century: Social, political, and economic challenges.* Baltimore, MD: JHU Press.

Anita Insights. (2024, June 21). *Building for serendipity at Google NYC.* Anita Insights Blog. Retrieved from: https://www.anitainsights.com/blog/building-for-serendipity-at-google-nyc/

Armstrong, N., & Chang, S. M. (2007). Location, location, location: Does seat location affect performance in large classes? *Journal of College Science Teaching, 37*(2), 54-58.

Astin, A. W. (1999). Student involvement: A developmental theory for higher education. *Journal of College Student Development, 40,* 518-529.

Bandura, A. (1997). *Self-efficacy: The exercise of control.* New York, NY: Freeman.

Baepler, P., & Walker, J. D. (2014). *Active learning spaces: New directions for teaching and learning.* San Francisco: Jossey-Bass.

Barker, R. G. (1965). Explorations in ecological psychology. *American Psychologist, 20*(1), 1-14.

Barker, R. G. (1965). *Exploration in ecological psychology.* Stanford University Press.

Beichner, R. J. (2014). History and evolution of active learning spaces. *International Journal of STEM Education,* 1(1), 1-11.

Bidwell, A. (2013, June 27a). Report: High school students have made no progress in 40 years. *U.S. News and World Report.* Retrieved from http://www.usnews.com/ news/articles/2013/06/27/report-high-school-students-have- made-no-progress-in-40-years

Bidwell, A. (2013, August 21b). High school graduates still struggle with college readiness. *U.S. News and World Report.* Retrieved from http://www.usnews.com/ news/articles/2013/08/21/high-school-graduates-still-struggle- with-college-readiness

Bingen, H. M., Aamlid, H. I., Hovland, B. M., Nes, A. A. G., Larsen, M. H., Skedsmo, K., Petersen, E. K., & Steindal, S. A. (2023). Use of active learning classrooms in health professional education: A scoping review. *International journal of nursing studies advances, 6,* 100167. https://doi.org/10.1016/j.ijnsa.2023.100167

Bohan, J. S. (1990). Social constructionism and contextual history: An expanded approach to the history of psychology. *Teaching of Psychology, 17*(2), 82-89.

Bonwell, C., & Eison, J. (1991). *Active learning: Creating excitement in the classroom AEHE-ERIC higher education reports.* Retrieved from ERIC database. (ED336049)

Brooks, D. C. (2011). Space matters: The impact of formal learning environments on student learning. *British Journal of Educational Technology, 42,* 719-726.

Brooks, D. C. (2012). Space and consequences: The impact of different formal learning spaces on instructor and student behavior. *Journal of Learning Spaces 1*(2), 1-8. Retrieved from http://libjournal.uncg.edu/index.php/jls/article/view/285/275

Brown, M., & Long, P. D. (2021, November 10). *The impact of learning space design on learner experience and collaboration. EDUCAUSE Review.* Retrieved from: https://er.educause.edu/articles/2021/11/the-impact-of-learning-space-design-on-learner-experience-and-collaboration

Bryant, R. T. A. (2015). *College preparation for African American students: Gaps in the high school educational experience.* Washington, DC: Center for Law and Social Policy (CLASP).

Caplan, R. D., & Harrison, R. V. (1993). Person-environment fit theory: Some history, recent developments, and future directions. *Journal of Social Issues, 49,* 253-275.

Carini, R. M., Kuh, G. D., & Klein, S. P. (2006). Student engagement and student learning: Testing the linkages. *Research in Higher Education, 47,* 1-32.

Chickering, A. W., & Gamson, Z. F. (1987). Seven principles for good practice in undergraduate education. *AAHE Bulletin, 39*(7), 3-7.

Cohen, A. M., & Kisker, C. B. (2007). *The shaping of American higher education: Emergence and growth of the contemporary system* (2nd ed.). San Francisco, CA: Jossey-Bass.

Cole, D. (2010). The effects of student-faculty interactions on minority students' college grades: Differences between aggregated and disaggregated data. *Journal of the Professoriate, 3*(2), 137-160.

Connolly, S., Flynn, E. E., Jemmott, J., & Oestreicher, E. (2017). First year experience for at-risk college students. *College Student Journal, 51*(1), 1-6.

Contreras, F. (2011). Strengthening the bridge to higher education for academically promising underrepresented students. *Journal of Advanced Academics, 22*, 500-526.

Deci, E. L., & Ryan, R. M. (1985). The general causality orientations scale: Self-determination in personality. *Journal of Research in Personality, 19*(2), 109-134.

Deloitte. (n.d.). *Deloitte University: A place for growth.* Deloitte South Africa. Retrieved From: https://www.deloitte.com/za/en/about/story/purpose-values/deloitte-university.html

Dewey, J. (1922). Education as engineering. *New Republic, 32*, 89-91.

Doll, B., Spies, R. A., LeClair, C. M., Kurien, S. A., & Foley, B. P. (2010). Student perceptions of classroom learning environments: Development of the ClassMaps survey. *School Psychology Review, 39*, 203-218.

Dori, Y. J., & Belcher, J. (2005). How does technology-enabled active learning affect undergraduate students' understanding of electromagnetism concepts? *The Journal of the Learning Sciences,* 14(2), 243-279.

Edmondson, A. C. (1999). *Psychological safety and learning behavior in work teams. Administrative Science Quarterly,* 44(2), 350–383.

Finney, J. E., Riso, C., Orosz, K., & Boland, W. C. (2014). *From master plan to mediocrity: Higher education performance and policy in California*. Philadelphia, PA: University of Pennsylvania Graduate School of Education. Retrieved from http://www.gse.upenn.edu/pdf/irhe/California_Report.pdf

Freeman, S., Eddy, S. L., McDonough, M., Smith, M. K., Okoroafor, N., Jordt, H., & Wedneroth, M. P. (2014). Active learning increases student performance in science, engineering, and mathematics. *Proceedings of the National Academic of Sciences.* Early edition available at http://www.pnas.org/content/early/2014/05/08/1319030111.full.pdf+html?sid=8c66e8e4-8eea-4989-b252-fab804e80328

Gallup. (2023). *State of the global workplace: 2023 report.* Washington, DC: Gallup, Inc.

Gaffney, J. D. H., Richards, E., Kustusch, M. B., Ding, L., & Beichner, R. J. (2008). Scaling up education reform. *Journal of College Science Teaching,* 37(5), 48-53.

Gensler. (n.d.). *Deloitte University.* Gensler. Retrieved from: https://www.gensler.com/projects/deloitte-university

Gilbreath, B., Kim, T., & Nichols, B. (2011). Person-environment fit and its effect on university students: A response surface methodology study. *Residential Higher Education, 52*(1), 47-62.

Goffe, W. L., & Kauper, D. (2014). A survey of principles instructors: Why lecture prevails. *The Journal of Economic Education, 45,* 360-375.

Harper, S. R. (2012). *Black male student success in higher education: A report from the National Black Male College Achievement Study.* Philadelphia, PA: University of Pennsylvania Graduate School of Education, Center for the Study of Race and Equity in Education.

Hausmann, L. R., Schofield, J. W., & Woods, R. L. (2007). Sense of belonging as a predictor of intentions to persist among African American and White first-year college students. *Research in Higher Education, 48,* 803-839.

Herman Miller. (n.d.). *Rethinking the classroom: How the design and furnishing of learning spaces can increase levels of engagement and foster active learning and teaching.*

Herman Miller Research White Paper. Retrieved from: https://www.hermanmiller.com/research/categories/white-papers/rethinking-the-classroom/

Hickman, L., Neubert, S., & Reich, K. (Eds.). (2009). *John Dewey between pragmatism and constructivism.* New York NY: Fordham University Press.

Hill, M., & Epps, K. (2010). The impact of physical classroom environment on student satisfaction and learning. *Learning Environments Research,* 13(3), 243-258.

IDEO. (2019, March 6). *How we designed a studio space that reflects our values.* IDEO Journal. Retrieved from: https://www.ideo.com/journal/how-we-designed-a-studio-space-that-reflects-our-values

IDEO. (n.d.). *Redesigning where we work and learn.* IDEO Works. Retrieved from: https://www.ideo.com/works/redesigning-where-we-work-and-learn

Kena, G., Aud, S., Johnson, F., Wang, X., Zhang, J., Rathbun, A., & Kristapovich, P. (2014). *The condition of education 2014* (NCES 2014-083). Washington, DC: National Center for Education Statistics.

Kim, Y. K., & Sax, L. J. (2017). The effects of student–faculty interaction on academic self-concept: Does academic major matter?. *Research in Higher Education, 55,* 780-809.

Kuh, G. D. (2003). What we're learning about student engagement from NSSE: Benchmarks for effective educational practices. *Change, 35*(2), 24-32.

Langer, E. J. (1997). *The power of mindful learning.* Reading, MA: Addison Wesley.

Livingston, J. (2011). *Defining and measuring faculty engagement: Validation of the Faculty Engagement Survey* (Doctoral dissertation). Azusa Pacific University Azusa, CA.

Lundberg, C. A. & Schreiner, L. A. (2004). Quality and frequency of faculty-student interaction as predictors of learning: An analysis by student race/ethnicity. *Journal of College Student Development, 45,* 549-565.

Michel, N., Cater, J. J., & Varela, O. (2009). Active versus passive teaching styles: An empirical study of student learning outcomes. *Human Resource Development Quarterly, 20,* 397-418.

Miller Dyer Spears Architects. (n.d.). *MIT TEAL classrooms.* MDS/Miller Dyer Spears Inc. Retrieved from: https://www.mds-bos.com/mit-teal-classrooms

Nakamura, J., & Csikszentmihalyi, M. (2005). Engagement in a profession: The case of undergraduate teaching. *Daedalus, 134*(3), 60-67.

National Assessment of Educational Progress (2025) - *The Nations Report Card.* Retrieved from: https://www.nationsreportcard.gov/

Piaget, J. (1964). Part I: Cognitive development in children: Piaget development and learning. *Journal of Research in Science Teaching, 2*(3), 176-186.

Rands, M. L., & Gansemer-Topf, A. M. (2017). *The room itself is active: How classroom design impacts student engagement. Journal of Learning Spaces, 6*(1). Retrieved from: https://files.eric.ed.gov/fulltext/EJ1152568.pdf

Ryan, R. M., & Deci, E. L. (2000). Self-determination theory and the facilitation of intrinsic motivation, social development, and well-being. *American Psychologist, 55*(1), 68-78.

Schreiner, L. A. (2010b). Thriving in the classroom. *About Campus, 15*(3), 2-10.

Schreiner, L. A. (2010b). The thriving quotient. In S. R. Harper & S. J. Quaye (Eds.), *Student Engagement in Higher Education* (pp. 41–62). Routledge.

Schreiner, L. A., & Louis, M. C. (2011). The engaged learning index: Implications for faculty development. *Journal on Excellence in College Teaching, 22*(1), 5-28.

Sinek, S. (2009). *Start with why: How great leaders inspire everyone to take action.* New York, NY: Portfolio.

Stamp, P. R. (2018). *The Role of Active Learning Pedagogy in First-Year Undergraduate College Students' Engaged Learning.* Azusa Pacific University.

Uline, C. L., Wolsey, T. D., Tschannen-Moran, M., & Lin, C. D. (2010). Improving the physical and social environment of schools. *Educational Administration Quarterly, 46*(1), 1-29.

Umbach, P. D., & Wawrzynski, M. R. (2005). Faculty do matter: The role of college faculty in student learning and engagement. *Research in Higher Education, 46,* 153-184.

University of Virginia Learning Design & Technology. (n.d.). *Active learning spaces.* Retrieved from: https://learningdesign.as.virginia.edu/space/active-learning-spaces

ViewSonic Education. (2023, May 17). *Integrating active learning spaces in modern classroom design: 3 essential pointers.* Retrieved from: https://www.viewsonic.com/library/education/integrating-active-learning-spaces-in-modern-classroom-design-3-essential-pointers/

Vygotsky, L. (1978). Interaction between learning and development. *Readings on the Development of Children, 23*(3), 34-41.

Wenderoth, M. P. (2014). Active learning increases student performance. *PNAS,* 111(23), 8410–8415.

Author Biography

Dr. Paula Raymond Stamp is a consultant, researcher, and educator whose work sits at the intersection of learning, leadership, and organizational culture. She is the founder of Geaux Consulting Group, where she advises executives, solopreneurs, small- to mid-size firms, and professional services teams on strategy, engagement, and the spaces that shape performance.

With a doctorate focused on active learning pedagogy and years of experience coaching leaders across industries, Paula brings a rare dual perspective: the academic depth to understand why people learn and behave the way they do, and the practical insight to help organizations turn that knowledge into measurable outcomes.

Her writing blends scholarship with real-world application, offering a fresh and accessible voice for anyone seeking to build environments where people think deeply, collaborate meaningfully, and thrive.

Paula lives in California, and writes about learning, leadership, and human connection.